SHAME
MONEY

Motunrayo Ade-Famoti

Printed in Nigeria by
Print Doctor Africa

@Moneystewards

@Moneystewards

@Moneystewards

@Moneystewards

Disclaimer

All erudition contained in this book is given for informational and educational purposes only. The author is in no way accountable for any results or outcomes that emanate from using this material. Constructive attempts have been made to provide information that is both accurate and effective, but the author is not responsible for the accuracy or use/misuse of this information.

Acknowledgments

I thank my Saviour Jesus Christ for the gift of love and life. I thank my husband, Ade Famoti for his unwavering support over the years. I thank my children for their unconditional love and prayers. I thank Yeye, my brothers and my sisters for always putting up with me. I thank my friends and mentees for being there for me. Lastly, I thank my mother, my mentor, my anchor and cheerleader, Comfort Titilayo Apata, who was the inspiration behind this book. Thanks for showing your children the essence of hard work and humility.

I dedicate this book to my late father, Ibukun Ayodele Apata. I miss you, I still long to hear your voice, and look forward to one more dance with you. God did answer your prayers because your baby girl turned out just fine. One day, I shall get to see you again. I love you forever.

Table of Contents

1

HELLO, SHAME MONEY!

"My name is Joyce. I used to be a medical doctor. Yes, you read that right, I used to be. I can't call myself a medical doctor now because I think I am too rusty to go back into the profession. You want to know my story? It is quite long, however, I will try to be as brief as possible.

I fell in love with the brother of one of my patients, and we ended up at the altar. My husband, who was trying to find his feet in the oil and gas sector, asked me to stop working at the hospital so I would have more time for the home. Initially, I did not agree but later gave in for the sake of peace.

My husband prospered in his business and gave me everything I needed. I toured the world with my children and dined with the high and mighty in the country. Life was good, or so I thought, even though I had no savings, much less investments!

About ten years into our marriage, my husband fell to the cold hands of death. It was then I discovered he had taken some bank loans. I was initially angry that he had kept such a secret from me, then I remembered how I had been busy spending his money lavishly. I became sober because I hadn't even cared to ask how his business was faring. The bank came after my family and we had to forfeit his company and some of his properties.

We had already sold some of his properties to keep up with our extravagance, and all we had left at that time was the house we were living in. I didn't want to sell it so my children and I wouldn't be homeless.

I knew I had to get a source of income quickly. Someone had once told me to start hairdressing on a commercial level because my daughters were always getting compliments on the hair I plaited for them. I thought to myself, "I think I should do this, but what will people say?" You think I was being proud, right? Well, maybe it is because you were not in my shoes.

The story above might be similar to yours, or not at all. If your monthly income is barely enough to cater for your needs, and you end up running into debt before the next paycheck, then this book is for you. Perhaps, you are in charge of your finances and you do not have any debt but you simply won't mind a second source of income to take care of petty needs or have extra cash to save every month, then this book is for you. Or it may be that you will be retiring soon and you don't have any other source of income to fall back on, then you must certainly continue to read this book.

Do you see yourself fall into any of these categories? Do not panic. The solution might just be Shame Money.

To attain financial security, I, Motunrayo, believe individuals should derive their income from a minimum of four sources:

Core Competence, Entrepreneurship, Consultancy & Partnerships, and Investments. This is linked to the instruction received by the first man in the Bible, Adam, in the garden. His duty was to oversee and tend the garden in Eden. To help him achieve this, God created a river to water the garden. This river was split into four streams: Euphrates, Gihon, Tigris, and Pishon.

Genesis 2:10 "Now a river flows from Eden to water the orchard, and from there it divides into four headstreams."

Pishon	Euphrates
Increase **Investment**	**Fruitfulness** **Core Competence**
Tigris	Gihon
Rapid **Consultancy** ***&*** **Partnerships**	**Bursting Forth** **Entrepreneurship**

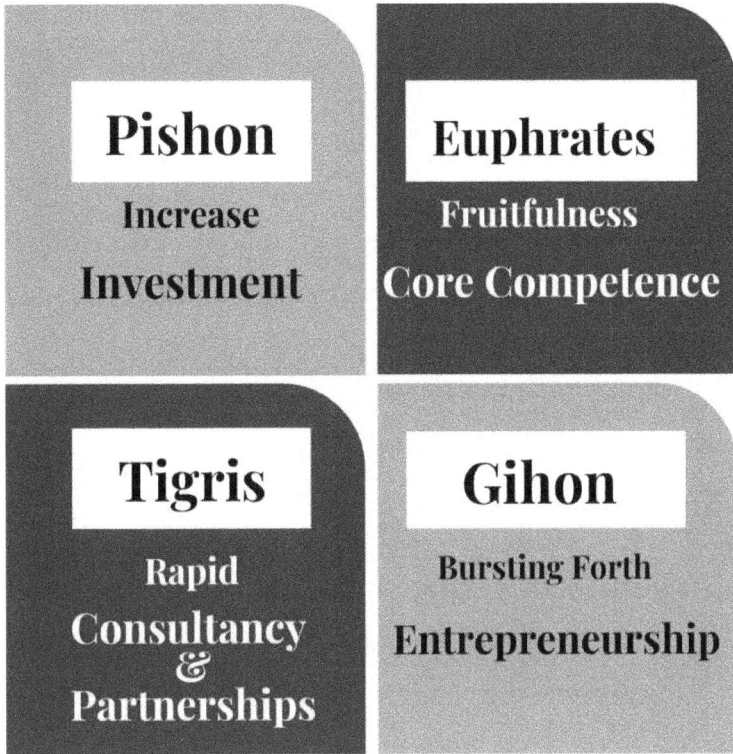

I have come to realize this: The four heads which the river is split into, represent four major streams of income. Just like the four heads of the river flowed in different directions, the four significant streams of income represent various sources of wealth in the world economy.

For more on the four streams of income, you can get my book on "Being a good Money Steward"

Core Competence is an area where you have gotten the requisite training to be able to practice on the job e.g. law, medicine, pharmacy.

Consultancy and Partnerships is being passively involved in another person's business. For example, you train staff in other firms outside your working hours or make referrals and earn a commission.

Investment involves investing a portion of your income into real estate or paper asset.

Entrepreneurship is setting up businesses with the aim of making profit. Here, the necessary skill, competence, or requisite capital might not be available; and that is where Shame Money comes in.

SHAME MONEY

Shame Money is what I describe as money you make shamefully. It is money you make from commercial sources that may initially seem below your competence, educational qualifications, or even your social status. You have a skill, gift, or talent that you can monetize but you are ashamed about what people will think or say.

You are a trained doctor but in need of extra income so, you begin to offer cleaning services. You are an engineer but also drive commercial buses. You are a lawyer but also offer catering services on the side. This side hustle is earning you some extra income and you can finally pay your bills and still have some money to save.

You may have friends snicker at you behind your back, or people perceive you to be less worthy because you have decided to pursue this venture. At its initial stage, you might even lose some friends who no longer want to associate with someone who is doing such a 'demeaning' job.

Although you may be embarrassed about Shame Money, it is important to note that Shame Money is neither illegal nor scandalous. Instead, it is empowering and confidence building. It builds tenacious character, a never-give-up and can-do spirit that one really needs to confront some of life's issues. It also helps ensure you uplift yourself through diligent hard work rather than relying on other people's handouts.

So many people have broken free from the shackles of poverty through various Shame Money ideas. Some have risen to fame by closing their ears to the 'opinions' of others and working their way through the shame to becoming leaders of empires. Some do not have an empire yet, but they are forever changed because they are now financially free and can even afford to employ other people.

Discover what your Shame Money idea is and name it. Now that you have named it, own the shame so you no longer need to be ashamed, and then 'fame it' … after all, 'shit money doesn't smell'. Raise your head up high, and do what you must do to survive. Then, make sure that you do not keep your business at the survival stage but build it to thrive.

At the end of each chapter in this book, there are some exercises that will help you review what you have learnt in the course of reading the chapter and also help you get started as a Shame Money entrepreneur.

I pioneered the concept of Shame Money and drew my inspiration from what I have seen and still see in society. I have put together some successful Shame Money stories to show this is not just my theory; it has worked for some people, and if it worked for them, it can work for you too.

ACTION POINTS

1. Have you ever heard about the Shame Money concept before now?

2. With the brief definition of Shame Money given in this chapter, do you know anyone currently implementing a Shame Money business idea? What was the first thing that came to mind when you heard that he/she was involved in such an enterprise?

3. Do you think it is something you can do?

4. Do you have a Shame Money idea of your own? If yes, why have you not started?

NOTES

2

MY SHAME MONEY HERO

I consider my mother, Mrs. Comfort Apata, to be my Shame Money hero. I do not give her this title just because she is my mother. She has earned it.

Born into a polygamous home in the South Western part of Nigeria, I would not say my mum was born into affluence. Her father was a cocoa farmer and her mother was a petty trader. Her father's status improved, and through diligence and hard work, he became a foremost cocoa merchant in his town before he died. Growing up, Mum always visited my grandfather's cocoa store, where she gradually started learning the principles of entrepreneurship.

After her secondary school education and with the requisite experience, she started work as a schoolteacher. In 1973, she got married to my dad and moved to Lagos. For the first three years of their marriage, she was a full-time housewife. My mum yearned for more. She didn't want to be home all day taking care of the kids. She wanted to work and earn some money and not totally depend on my dad for her finances.

She couldn't get a corporate job as she had no university education and could not get a loan to start a business because she didn't have any asset to use as collateral. When she told my dad about her desire to work, he told her to be patient as something was going to come up soon.

Her first shot at Shame Money

One day, she went to Agege market in Lagos, Nigeria, to get foodstuff and saw some beautiful 'Made in America' dresses. One of my sisters would soon be celebrating her birthday, so my mum bought two dresses for ₦7 each.

When she got home, she looked at the dresses closely and it occurred to her that the dresses might be worth more than the amount she got them for. She thought for one moment about possibly selling the dresses for profit. After thinking about it for a while, she decided to at least give it a try.

She took the dresses to her friend, Mrs. James, who also had daughters the clothes would fit. She admired them and asked my mum where she got them from. My mother, not wanting to sound cheap, told Mrs. James that she had bought them from an aunt who had just come back from America. Mrs. James asked if she was willing to sell the clothes. My mum replied, "No problem."

"So, how much do each of this cost?" Mrs. James asked.

My mum only knew what she had paid for those clothes, but she blurted out the first figure that came to her mind. "Each goes for ₦10," she said.

Mrs. James did not bargain or ask for a discount. She simply went into her room, brought out the money and gave it to my mum. Elated, mum headed home. On her way, so many thoughts went through her mind. She couldn't believe she had just earned a profit of almost ₦6 for a few hours' work. She got home and did the math. Transport fare to and from the market and back to her house to buy the clothes was ₦0.40k. So, she had made a profit of ₦5.60 by just selling two dresses at a friend's house!

She went back to the market and got more clothes. She took them to another friend of hers, Mrs. Taibat, who was a civil servant and an entrepreneur who sold clothes and shoes in her shop. Mum went to her house and showed her the dresses. "My aunty just got back from America and she brought these dresses. Would you be interested in buying them from me so you can sell to people at your office?"

Mrs. Taibat took the dresses from her and examined them. She was stunned. "Wow, these are beautiful dresses. How much are you selling them?" Mum went for the kill. "₦12 each."

"That's not a problem. I will buy all you have brought today, and I wouldn't mind you getting about ten more pieces for me," Mrs. Taibat responded.

To say my mum was thrilled would have been an understatement. She was still reeling from joy when one of Mrs. Taibat's neighbours came in. She commented on how beautiful the dresses were and asked for their prices. Mrs. Taibat did not allow my mum to speak. She said, "I bought them from her at ₦18 apiece. I will sell it for ₦25."

"Please, sell to me for ₦18," her neighbour pleaded. "No way! I will sell each for ₦25," Mrs. Taibat responded.

Mum was shocked. While she knew that people loved American products because they believed they were of superior quality, she did not know the dresses would sell for that much. She went back to her house, thinking of where she would get the money to buy the additional ten dresses Mrs. Taibat ordered. She summoned up courage and went back to the seller in Agege market. She knelt in front of the seller, pleading and asking to purchase some of the goods she wanted on credit. The clothes seller refused. She did not know my mother intimately and was worried she would abscond with the clothes.

After much pleading, the seller looked at my mum who was still on her knees and said, "You look responsible.

You have to understand, there are a lot of bad people out there, but if I close my eyes because a bad person is passing by, my eyes might still be shut when a good person is passing by."

She told my mum she would only give her six dresses and not the ten she requested for. Mum was grateful. She took the six dresses to Mrs. Taibat who paid immediately. My mum paid the clothes seller as promised and reinvested the profit in buying extra clothes. Having earned her trust, the seller gave her six more dresses on credit. This continued until all of Mrs. Taibat's orders were fulfilled.

This was my mum's first attempt at entrepreneurship, and she made ₦300 from that entire transaction. That was a lot of money in the late 70s. In trying to figure out a way to expand and structure her new business, she decided to save the money she had made and use it as capital for her next venture.

There was a high demand for foreign products at the time. This led to another thought. What if she bought stuff from the market and took them to offices to sell? With the ₦300, she went to the Lagos Island market and bought clothes, shoes and bags. She then took the items to some offices at Ikeja.

She made friends with receptionists at these offices and even gave them some items for free. The receptionists would go in and ask the people in the office if they wanted to buy what my mum was selling. Though they would mostly buy on credit and pay at the end of the month, Mum continued this business. Soon, she began to add more products to her list, and at one point, she was selling almost everything her customer requested.

ACTION POINTS

1. How daring are you when it comes to making money legitimately?

```
┌─────────────────────────────────────────┐
│                                         │
├─────────────────────────────────────────┤
│                                         │
├─────────────────────────────────────────┤
│                                         │
├─────────────────────────────────────────┤
│                                         │
└─────────────────────────────────────────┘
```

2. What are the worst comments you think people might say if they see you executing your Shame Money idea? Write them out below.

```
┌─────────────────────────────────────────┐
│                                         │
├─────────────────────────────────────────┤
│                                         │
├─────────────────────────────────────────┤
│                                         │
├─────────────────────────────────────────┤
│                                         │
└─────────────────────────────────────────┘
```

3. Face your "fear of the shame" by writing out your honest response to such comments.

| |
| |
| |
| |
| |

I am deeply passionate about helping others discover their Shame Money ideas. To date, I have helped tons of people navigate through their shame and come out on top. Would you like to identify the source of your Shame Money?

Then you can sign up for my online course by visiting the website address below to become part of the Shame Money online community.

www.shamemoney.com

NOTES

3

NO GOING BACK ON SHAME MONEY

When my dad noticed my mum's diligence and hard work in her business, he introduced her to a Chinese man, Mr. Chan Lee.

Mr. Lee worked at a rubber company, SOPACO, which manufactured bathroom slippers. At the company, she was told she had to register as a distributor before they could give her bathroom slippers to sell. The cost of registration was ₦2,000.

At the time, my mum was ready to pursue this line of business; but where on earth would she get ₦2,000? She spoke to my dad about getting the money although she knew he also could not afford it.

He went back to speak with Mr. Chan Lee who agreed to ₦1,000 registration because of their relationship. Mum was somewhat relieved; she only had to look for half of the amount that the company initially requested for.

She approached her sister and asked for part of the money, while requesting they forge a partnership. Her sister declined the partnership but agreed to give her the money. She was not interested in selling bathroom slippers because she considered it demeaning. She preferred to sell lace materials.

Mum would not be deterred. She would rather do this than be a stay-at-home mum. Many years later, she would build her first house with the proceeds from selling bathroom slippers.

There Is No Shame in My Game

After she took the money from her sister and registered with SOPACO, they gave her the first batch of slippers. She did not have a shop, so she took everything home.

With her entrepreneurial spirit, mum took her slippers from one place to the other, but people were not as interested in the slippers as they were in the dresses. For three months, my mum could not sell half of the products. There were neither cell phones nor internet and hardly any landlines at that time. So, she would go around with samples and give retailers her address so they could come to the house to buy from her. So many people promised to come to the house, but none showed up.

It was a very tough period for my mum because other distributors were collecting goods worth ₦4,000 each from SOPACO, selling all their goods and getting huge commissions. My mother, who had borrowed money to make up the ₦1,000 to invest, could not even sell enough goods to get at least a quarter of the commission others were getting.

When I asked my mum, what kept her going during such periods, she simply said it was because she loved what she was doing. She needed to stay focused to be able to pay back the debt and ultimately contribute to the family economy. She was so sure things were going to work out, so she kept pushing towards success.

In my mother's words, "If you are passionate about what you are doing, God will bring people who will help you." When people see you doing something and doing it well, they will try to see what they can do to assist you. However, you must take the first step. The first step might be hard and it might be 'shameful'; people might not even believe in what you intend to do, however, if you will brace up and take that first step, you will find other things falling in place for you.

If you are doing something one way, and you are not getting results, maybe it is time to try doing it another way.

My mum knew things could not continue this way. She thought of several ways to sell those slippers and eventually came up with a strategy. She went to the retailers at Agege market and asked them where they got the slippers they were selling.

They said they got theirs from the Lagos Island market. She told them she had precisely the same quality of goods they were selling and was willing to sell it to them at the same amount they got it in Lagos Island. The retailers agreed to buy from her. Their only condition was that they could not come to her house.

She told them that was not a problem as she would bring her goods to the market. The next day, she got a taxi and headed straight for the market.

She offloaded her goods at a spot in the market, took some samples and went around meeting the retailers again. The responses she received were good. 'This looks good. Give me ten pairs.' 'May I have six pairs?' 'Will you give me a dozen pieces now and collect the payment next week?'

While some of them did not pay immediately, over some weeks and months, after many persistent reminders, my mum eventually got all the money back. Finally, she was able to sell off the entire first batch of slippers!

Providence

On one of her trips to Agege market, she met an elderly man whom she simply called Baba (an elderly person in this part of the world, Nigeria, is often referred to as "Baba"). He turned out to be who you can call a destiny helper. She walked into Baba's shop and showed him some samples.

"Young lady, I just got back from Lagos Island. As you can see, my shop is well stocked. I need to sell everything off before I buy new ones," Baba said, trying to dismiss her. Mum was undeterred. "No problem, Baba. The next time you need to restock your shop, please patronize me".

"I will sell the goods to you at the same price you get them at Lagos Island, or even cheaper."

Baba looked at her curiously. Mum was still in her twenties. He saw the passion with which she went about her business and asked her where her shop was.

"I don't have a shop, Baba. I bring my goods to the market in buses and taxis every day, and when I am done selling, I take what is left back to the house."

He was silent for a while and then he said, "Do you see that store over there? You can start using it for now. You don't have to take your goods back to the house every day from now on. You can keep them there."

My mum could not believe her ears. Kneeling, with tears in her eyes and a joyful shout, she screamed, "Thank you, Baba. I am so grateful. God bless you forever". She had gotten a store just like that! That was a breakthrough for her.

From Agege to Lagos Island

My mum did not just focus on selling at the Agege market alone; periodically, she took her goods to the Lagos Island market and sold to people there.

How did she start selling in the Lagos Island market? She noticed that whenever she got to the bathroom slippers factory, SOPACO, there were people who would always come with big trucks each week to buy goods. She wondered who their customers were and how they could sell that much within a week. She approached one of them who was from the south-eastern part of the country. He would come to Lagos, buy slippers and take them down to Onitsha to sell. He would also take some to the Lagos Island market to sell.

Mum asked him if he had buyers in Lagos that could buy from her. Well, he did something that might be uncommon these days. He took her to his customers in Lagos Island and introduced her to them. He told them to buy from her also, as she always had good products. He was exceedingly kind to her, and she returned the favor by giving him several gifts. Mum had a good relationship with the staff of SOPACO and maintained a good relationship with all her contacts.

SOPACO had different brands of slippers, some of which would sell faster than the others. Some of the staff would give my mother more of those that sold faster, and she would in turn, pass the tip on to the south- eastern man. It was a good business deal! Everyone was happy.

Shame Money is not an easy thing to do, but if you can get over the shame and look within, you will discover you have an advantage: a gift, a skill, or a passion you can monetize. Summon the courage, start your Shame Money idea, and grow it into a business. I believe God has never created anyone without giving them a unique gift or talent. You must find yours, develop it, and harness it. Don't be afraid to ask for help when you need it. If someone does not assist you, another person will.

No man is an island in life and especially in business. You will need people to help you and open doors for you. The need for you to be open to the help of others cannot be overstated. What is much more powerful than the viability of your Shame Money business idea is your openness to collaborating with other people. This can only be done effectively to propel your business if you develop the will to help others and to also receive help from other people.

When you need the push to the next level in your business, what God does is to send you people that have the keys to the door you are trying to open. So, choose to see them and let them help you when they offer their help.

Don't be afraid to ask for help or to receive it!

As you kick start your Shame Money journey, be kind, honest and compassionate to everyone you meet. Please do not get me wrong, I am not asking you to let people trample all over you and cheat you. What I am saying is, your innate kindness and honesty will be more favorable to you and your business, sooner than you think.

Growing your business is going to be so much easier if you can cultivate this value.

ACTION POINTS

1. List out the major steps you need to take to start or grow your Shame Money business.

2. How will partnerships help you get there faster?

NOTES

4

INTEGRITY WILL TAKE YOU FARTHER

My mum's business was gradually becoming successful, and she was now making lots of money. However, being in the market, she could not physically count the cash due to security reasons. In those days, everyone dealt with cash. There were no ATMs, credit cards, mobile monies and transfers like we have today.

She would collect whatever cash each customer had given her, write their name and amount they claimed to have given to her on a piece of paper, tie it together with the money and put it in her money box. She would then take everything home and count each customer's money individually.

One day, after getting home, she went to her room to count her money and discovered that a woman, Alhaja, had overpaid her by ₦1. She was supposed to pay ₦100 but had paid ₦101.

The next morning, she went to the woman's shop. The following conversation ensued.

Mum: Alhaja, I came back because of the money you gave to me yesterday….

Alhaja: *(cutting her short)* Young lady, don't even start. I did not short change you. I paid you the correct amount. Don't tell me that I didn't give you the total amount of money….

(Mum allowed her to finish her tirade.)

Mum: Alhaja, I was trying to say that you overpaid me. Here is your ₦1.

(Mum stretched out her hand to give Alhaja the ₦1.)

Alhaja: Hmm. So, there are honest people everywhere. Where is your shop?

Mum: I don't have a shop here in Lagos Island. I bring my goods in buses and taxis every time.

Alhaja: So, you came all the way to Lagos Island market because of ₦1?

Mum: Yes.

Alhaja: How much is your return transport fare to the market?

Mum: 60k. Alhaja was shocked. (100 kobo make one naira).

My mother also inculcated the habit of honesty in her siblings who she brought to Lagos to work with her. "Never take what does not belong to you," she would often say. "And if a customer overpays you, don't keep quiet. Give back the balance."

Alhaja vowed to assist my mum in securing a shop in Lagos Island because of her integrity. Of her own volition, she informed the head of the market association and the traders agreed to get her a shop in the market. My mum was told of their offer, and she told my dad about it, but he blatantly refused. Dad felt that getting a second shop would make her come home late in the evenings and consequently affect the children's stability.

My mum told the traders that she could not have a shop in the market. All she could have (and all she had till she stopped selling at that market) was a storage unit to store her goods, so she wouldn't have to take them home every day. She did not return her unsold goods to the house like she used to do but was able to keep them in the storage unit.

There was a high level of trust, at the time, amongst the sellers in the market. She could also leave the store keys with the traders and not take them home. As a result, they would also help to sell her items when she could not make it to the market!

I remember growing up, Mum would sometimes take us to the market. Always extremely busy, she never really explained much about her business. However, one thing I knew was that she and her sisters left the house at 4 a.m. in the mornings to go and sell goods in the market. In the evenings, they would come back home with cash and we would all help to count the money. I understood that hard work was sooner or later going to be rewarded.

When I got into university, my mum encouraged me to invest in stocks and real estate. She would tell my friends and I about several opportunities she missed in real estate and encourage us to start investing early. When I started working, she helped me buy my first piece of land and stocks. Although I was just 20 years old, I had started my investment journey and was looking forward to becoming a seasoned investor one day.

Shame Money Continues to Expand

My dad, during his course of work, met an Indian man, Mr. Batacharyah. During one of their many conversations, he asked my dad what Mum did for a living. Dad responded, "Buying and selling goods."

"That is good. I work at a textile factory. Can she become one of our distributors?" Mr. Batacharyah asked. At that point, my dad had come to appreciate Mum's business skills and was confident she would succeed as a distributor of a large company. "I am sure she would like to. I will talk to her about it and get back to you."

Trust my mother not to say no to opportunities. "Well, I have never tried selling fabrics before, but I would sure like to try. My experience in selling slippers should be of help. I think I will give it a shot."

She went with my dad to Mr. Batacharyah's office at

I.T.I Textile Company and that was it. She began her foray into the textile world. Mr. Batacharyah gave her some samples which she took around the market. She did the market survey herself and realized the demand for school check (material used for making school uniforms) was higher than the demand for other fabrics.

Consequently, she sold more of school checks than other fabrics. During the '80s, the government of the day banned the importation of some products because they could be produced locally, and so local production grew. As domestic production grew, so did the demand for local products.

On market days, when we were not going to school, Mum would wake my siblings and me up, and we would follow our aunts to the Aswani market in Lagos. We usually left the house at about 4 a.m. We would display the fabrics and help our aunts to sell them. It was a very lucrative business because people from other African countries came to Nigeria to buy fabrics.

There was no cashless transaction at the time, so everybody came to the market with cash. Mum would come to where we were stationed at 8am and two or three big sacks would have been filled with money. She would carry the sacks to the textile industry and buy more fabrics to be sold the next market day.

Whilst selling the bathroom slippers, she had saved enough money from the business to buy a pickup van. This made it easy for her to move around with her fabrics and get more to sell.

There was no need for her to hire taxis whenever she

was going to the market again. She drove this pickup van herself for three years before she got a driver.

Oppositions? Yes.

When Mum started selling fabrics, she met Mrs. Funmi, who was also a fabric seller. Mrs. Funmi had been the sole distributor of school checks and ran a monopoly. As a result, she made a lot of money from sales. She got to know Mr. Batacharyah had brought in my mum and wasn't pleased about it. The first batch of goods that Mum got from the factory was ten rolls of fabric. As she was about to leave with the fabric, Mrs. Funmi came in, and there was an exchange of words between her and my mother.

Mum would not be threatened. She went ahead to sell the fabric and returned to the factory to get more rolls.

My mum intimated my dad on what happened on her first day at the textile factory, and he advised that they reported it to the General Manager. To resolve the issue, I.T.I Textile Company had a management meeting after which they summoned the two women. Mrs. Funmi was told the company could not afford to continue with her being the only distributor; they had to bring in more people.

They introduced a sharing ratio, 60:40, with the larger share in favour of Mrs. Funmi.

Mum appreciated the gesture and asked if they could divide her share in two: she would only buy 20% while the company would allow other distributors to come in and buy 20% directly from them. The management staff at the company were happy with the idea. Other distributors were also happy because they could make more profit, but all this further infuriated Mrs. Funmi. After a while, Mum prayed about the situation and made several attempts to establish a friendship with Mrs. Funmi. She also helped Mrs. Funmi to transport her goods to the Lagos Island market.

In no time, they became friends. When my mum wanted to invest in real estate in Ikorodu, Lagos, it was Mrs. Funmi who helped her to source for a piece of land. Mum ended up not buying it because my dad felt Ikorodu was too far from their main residence.

Back in those days, distributors created their own designs. Mum created several designs for other fabrics when school checks were not so much in high demand and she made a lot of money from the sale of her designs.

There was a copyright on these designs which the factory would produce exclusively for the creator of the design. Selling your designs to others was a violation of your copyright, a practice the sellers did not engage in. If you had exceptionally beautiful designs and was particularly good at selling them fast, you had a window of opportunity to make very good money. If you were not fast enough, chances were that someone else could copy your designs and take them to another factory to register as theirs.

More connections to other textile companies

My mum took her journey further from I.T.I Textile Company to FIVE STAR Textile Industry, thanks to my father who again introduced her to Mr. Yadouf, who worked at the company. From these connections, she was able to also build connections with other textile companies, and this really helped expand her business.

In all, Mum became a distributor for about five textile companies when she was into active sales.

This chapter of my mom's story truly emphasizes the importance of networking and partnerships in growing your business.

When you have a strong vision of where you intend to take

your business to, it will show in the intentional steps you take to continuously grow the business.

A fire burning in your heart for your business growth can always be detected by the people around you, because you won't be able to stop talking about it, praying about it and doing something about it. This strong force in your heart will attract help from the people in your network. When an opportunity comes up you will most likely be the first person they will think of and recommend.

You are not being proud when you dream big and take big steps. Adversaries to your growth will come just like Mrs. Funmi vehemently stood against my mom's growth in the business, but your resolve to succeed must be stronger. Never dim your light to make anyone more comfortable or less irritated. Instead, shine brighter.

ACTION POINTS

1. What are your values? How committed are you to them?

   Do you believe honesty is an integral part of running businesses?

   | |
   | |
   | |
   | |
   | |

2. What are the likely challenges that you envisage in your Shame Money journey?

   | |
   | |
   | |
   | |
   | |

3. How do you intend to work your way around these
   challenges?

4. What if the business fails the first time you try?
   What are your plans for recovery?

NOTES

5

PATIENCE WILL KEEP YOU ON THE JOB

It took Mum seven years to build her house with the proceeds she made from the sale of bathroom slippers. Gratification is not usually instant if you want to succeed as an entrepreneur; you might not start making a lot of money immediately. Patience is key.

In the beginning, and subsequently, you should expect to stumble and make mistakes which might cost you a lot monetarily. What will keep you on the job, help you focus on the end goal, and stop you from being complacent is patience, perseverance, and faith.

She Struck Gold Selling Cement!

In 1992, Mum started selling cement. One of her elder cousins, a registered distributor with one of the cement factories in Nigeria, encouraged her to try it out. He felt she would make more money selling cement than fabrics.

At the cement factory, only registered distributors could go into the factory to buy bags of cement. Others had to buy from the distributors. My mum was not a registered distributor, so she had to buy from the distributors, especially her cousin. The distributors were making a profit of ₦5 to ₦10 per bag.

She soon discovered it was easier to get into the cement factory during the rainy season. This was because construction was usually very low during such periods, and due to less demand, prices would be cheaper. She decided to buy cement during rainy seasons and sell during dry seasons when demand would be high. She also hoped for an extra gain of ₦10 per bag above the usual profit she would make during dry seasons.

One rainy season, she bought three thousand bags at ₦510,000 (₦170 per bag). When the dry season came, which was peak period, the factory stopped selling and the price of cement went up. Surprisingly, she sold her inventory of cement for ₦1,290,000 (₦430 per bag). She had made a profit of over 150%!

She decided to make a major investment in the cement business, so she bought a used trailer and went into the supply of gypsum. By the time she was retiring from active sales, she owned eight trailers.

Mum later discovered that profits from the sale of textiles were almost the same as those from the sale of cement, so she continued selling both.

My Mum Got Swindled!

My mother's Shame Money story was not all rosy, so don't expect yours to be. You should prepare for losses, downfalls, and betrayals. However, you should also have plans in place to get up when you are knocked down and keep these occurrences to the barest minimum.

Mum owned a shop, which was managed by one of her sisters, where she sold alcoholic and non-alcoholic drinks. She was buying and reselling one hundred crates of drinks from Coca-Cola every week.

The way it worked was that a staff of Coca-Cola would come to the market once a week with products and supply to whoever wanted the products. You will give the Coca-Cola staff the money for the drinks and indicate your order on your purchase card.

One day, my mum gave some money to her sister, Adunni, to buy the drinks when the Coca-Cola products came. She also gave her the purchase card. Adunni wanted to leave the shop, so she, in turn, gave the money and the card to my grandmother and she left.

According to the story, a fair lady who was well dressed, came to my grandmother, and introduced herself as my mother's friend. She came with a small boy who had some pineapples in a tray. She introduced him as her son. This fair lady sat down comfortably in the shop, took one pineapple from the boy, sliced it, and gave it to my grandmother who put in the fridge.

She told my grandmother that the staff of Coca-Cola had left the street and were on their way out. She requested my granny to give her the money so she could give it to them, and they could come back to supply the drinks. My grandmother believed the fair lady was truly my mother's friend, so she gave her the money and the purchase card. The fair lady left the shop with the boy, leaving what was left of his goods in the shop. That was the last my grandmother saw of her.

When my mum got back to the shop, my grandmother asked if she had seen her friend who had just come to collect the money for the drinks. My mum folded her hands and put them on her head as she realized they had been swindled. "I did not tell any of my friends to come to the shop. You have been duped" she said.

"It is not possible. The fair lady came with her son. Look at his wares over there," my grandmother said, pointing to the pineapples on the tray. Mum looked at the pineapples and the tray. If they sold everything on the tray, the money realized would not buy one bottle of Coca-Cola drink. So much loss!

Just then, the boy came back and handed over the purchase card to my grandmother while asking for some money.

"Where is your mum?" My grandmother barked at him. The news had gone around, and a crowd had gathered in front of the shop. "She is not my mum," he said, crying. "I was just hawking, and she called me to follow her to her shop, and she brought me here. I followed her to collect my money, but she entered a taxi. She gave me this card to give to Mama and told me that Mama would give me the money for the pineapple she put in Mama's fridge."

My grandmother became teary eyed. "Don't cry, Mum," my mum consoled her. "This is business and this kind of thing happens."

It was quite an experience but that would not be all. There would still be more encounters with swindlers.

On one other occasion, some people had come to one of Mum's shops in a Toyota Hiace bus and told the manager, who was my mum's sister, that my mother had told them to bring some goods from the shop. At the time, there were no mobile phones. So, there was no way to call my mother to confirm this. The manager gave them the goods and that was the end of it. They were never seen again.

How was my mother able to manage so many shops at the same time?

My mother ran an empire that spanned a chain of business enterprises spread across Lagos, Nigeria. She sold ready-to-wear items, bathroom slippers, cement, fabrics, beverages, etc. To oversee each, she brought in her siblings and other family members from the village and put them in charge of her shops. Sometimes she hired managers to oversee each location.

Building good relationships is very germane to Shame Money. At inception, you might need some services you cannot afford financially. Relationships you have built over the years can come in handy in meeting those needs. You might not have all the millions you need to grow the business, but with the help of honest and amazing people, you can grow at a consistent pace. One day, you will look back and wonder how all the puzzles fit to create the phenomenal business you pictured in your mind.

In business you will encounter setbacks. Oh yes! If it was all a "rosy" journey, everyone will be Jeff Bezos.

Your strength will be tested. You will lose money. People will steal from you. You will be betrayed.

The first female self-made millionaire in America, Madam C.J Walker, built a great business from the ground up. Most of her troubles came from the betrayal of the people she trusted the most and competitors turn adversaries. You might have heard that the business world is not for the faint-hearted, it is true! There are sharks and wolves waiting for the slightest opportunity to pounce and crumble what you are building. So, brace yourself!

This is not to make you paranoid but to prepare you for the reality of the business world outside of the pages of this book.

When you face such challenges, address the weakness in your business structure, learn the lesson and persevere. A resilient spirit is a great treasure to have.

'The greater the risk, the greater the profit' is an economic law that does not always apply in entrepreneurship'. Low risks can sometimes result in huge profits. However, risk-taking is necessary for successful entrepreneurship. You cannot hide from it.

ACTION POINTS

1. How prepared are you to take RISKS?

| |
| |
| |

2. What potential risk can you detect in your
Shame Money business idea?

| |
| |
| |

3. How do you intend to overcome them?

| |
| |
| |
| |
| |

NOTES

6

MANAGING MULTIPLE BUSINESSES ALONGSIDE THE HOME

If you ask some women why they have abandoned their dreams, goals, and pursuits, the answer would be, "I had to give them all up to take care of my
children. I am making a sacrifice for the children."

Hello young woman, please ditch that excuse. It does not work anymore. You can take good care of your family and still make an impact except you have health challenges that will not allow that, or you are not physically strong enough.

My mum had five children. Despite her businesses and managing all her shops, she still took care of the home. In fact, she cooked all the meals every day.

How did she do it?

She would get up early in the morning and make breakfast for everyone in the family. My father hardly ate breakfast at home; instead, he took it to work. My mum, or any of her sisters living with us, would get the children ready for school and afterwards go to the shops. She enrolled us in an after-school program that was being run by one of our teachers, and we would be at the teacher's house until evening when my mum would come to pick us up.

We all made sacrifices to make the system work. While she would have loved to spend more time with us, it would have meant she would not have been able to build a strong business that would eventually contribute to her children's foreign education - an education which gave me the platform to run an international company today.

A woman should contribute to the family's economy. Today's expenses in most cases cannot be borne by the man alone. Everything is a lot more expensive than it used to be.

A few excuses given by women for not contributing to the family economy;

"I want to stay at home and take care of my children."

This is completely appreciated. While you should stay with your kids, especially when they are young, you must remain productive. There are several jobs, work opportunities and businesses you can take advantage of from home.

You can also sign up for my online course and be a part of the online community on www.shamemoney.com This course explains how you can start a new business and launch it in 14 days. The online community will continue to give you practical tips and support as you start and scale up your Shame Money business.

"My husband does not want me to work."

This is a common and disheartening issue in some families. It is best to understand why your husband does not want you to go out to work and see if you can make him see reason.

Having counseled a lot of women, some reasons for this excuse range from personality flaws to old-fashioned cultural and religious beliefs. Examples of personality flaws are that the woman will become independent, promiscuous, proud, rude, insubordinate, not submissive, etc. If these are his reasons, start your business at home using our online course on Shame Money and join the Shame Money community.

Warning: Never become complacent while staying at home or do nothing simply because of your husband and kids. You will soon become stagnant, frustrated, resentful and unproductive. Your kids will grow up and leave you at home, and your husband who didn't want you to work will remind you in the future of how you have become obsolete and not contributed to the family income. Unfortunately, this is the reality a lot of women find themselves in.

If your husband is able and willing to provide all you need, then that is very good. I will still encourage you to create opportunities for yourself because family finances may sometimes take a turn for the worse. However, if the family lives from paycheck to paycheck, with little savings and no substantial real estate or investment, it means your family needs your financial contribution and you need to provide it.

"I don't have enough entrepreneurial skills."

Many of us did not have such skills when we started. We had to acquire the necessary skills through reading, learning, and gleaning from past experiences. Any skill can be learnt or acquired. By joining the right community, you will be able to learn from other people's experiences and build the right support system and accountability program for yourself.

Like anything in life, you will need to take calculated risks. However, you must know that life never promises certainties.

Entrepreneurship is not for the risk-averse

Mum's journey into real estate started after she heard of her sister's encounter with armed robbers inside a bank, despite the intense security! This was a harrowing experience for my mum. It was then that she decided she was going to transform some of her liquid assets into fixed assets. She was going to get the necessary knowledge and invest in lands and buildings. She did this and recorded monumental successes in real estate.

Sometime in 1998, one of her relatives told her that he had been told to market a piece of land in Garki, Abuja, Nigeria and it was going for ₦1,200,000 which, at the time, was a lot of money. Though Abuja was the nation's capital, it was still underdeveloped. Still, my mum saw it as a good investment. She knew that because it was the nation's capital, investments in Abuja would eventually pay off.

My mother flew with one of my sisters to Abuja. After inspecting the land, which was quite large, she made the payment. The owner further explained to my mum, that prior to my mum buying the property, he had obtained a planning approval to build six flats on the property and would not mind selling the approval to my mum. She asked him for the cost, and he said it was ₦750,000. Mum paid for it and took possession of the land.

About four months later, her relative called her again. "Do you mind selling that piece of land? Someone is offering ₦4,000,000 for it." My Mum could not believe her ears. That was double the amount she had invested in the piece of land

and the offer was coming within four months of her purchase. "Please, tell the person that I am not selling," she told him.

Not too long afterwards, the relative called again and tried to convince my mum to sell because some people were mounting pressure on him to sell to them. My mum knew that her investment was surely going to pay off in the end, so she said no.

In 2002 (four years after she bought the property), she got another call. This time it was for her to sell at ₦55,000,000. She chose not to sell but went on to construct a building on the land.

Would my mum have considered herself lucky?

Well, yes and no. If you were to ask her, she would answer by saying that, indeed, God favored her. Back in the day, the economic atmosphere was favorable to entrepreneurs and she took advantage of that. She also was privileged to get some links through my father's influence. She considers herself blessed.

However, she also played her part. She was a go-getter who wouldn't take no for an answer. She was determined never to give up. She put in a lot of hard work, and God blessed her efforts.

"If you are not ready to take risks, don't bother going into entrepreneurship."

That was my mum talking to a millennial who had come to her to talk about her business. "Entrepreneurship is all about taking risks. Believe that the best will happen but prepare for the worst."

She also has this advice for young ones: "Entrepreneurship will take you far. Don't just consider getting a job, think of creating jobs; think ahead, think forward. If you look at the African economy now, you will see that the future is in manufacturing and agriculture. In fact, I have started a farm and very soon, I should be supplying food to thousands of people in the country".

"Be patient; good things do not come fast. Be committed to your work, be hardworking. Be interested in what you are doing. Don't go into it just for the money, go into it because it is what you love doing. You might not have the kind of opportunities I had back then, but this period provides different and maybe even better opportunities. You cannot stumble into wealth. You must work your way into it. Be careful about who you take advice from. Some of them are good, but some will not let you achieve your goals. There are times you would need to shut your ears to what people are saying so you can be focused."

My own Shame Money Experience

A few years ago, I was an Assistant Vice President and Head of Department at a top financial services company in Nigeria. Though the salary was good, I started my own Shame Money business by selling smoothies to my colleagues and other staff members. When I started, it was really embarrassing for me to sell smoothies for ₦200 but I continued all the same.

People could not comprehend why someone in my position would decide to sell smoothies, and some of them even made condescending remarks. I refused to be deterred because I had a passion for it. I knew I had to start small and work my way up. I also knew it was a business, and I had to treat it with the respect it deserved.

Once I overcame the shame, the smoothie business took off and the rewards started to come. Shortly afterwards, I was relieved of my duties at the financial institution. Thankfully, I had saved a bit of money. Using the proceeds from my Shame Money business and income saved from my salary and partnerships, I started my investment business.

The persuasive skill I developed while marketing my smoothies has greatly contributed to my success now as a real estate investor. Now, I don't convince people to buy a product of ₦200 but products worth millions of dollars. Same skill, different product. Today, my company, Moneystewards, which has developed multi- million-dollar real estate projects, has a presence in the United States, United Kingdom and Africa.

Simply put, I named it, shamed it, and famed it!

ACTION POINTS

I believe that a woman really has no excuse to be mediocre. If you are a woman but think you cannot do as advised above, please answer the following questions and email your answers to info@moneystewards.org, I would love to hear from you.

1. How do you intend to combine what you do currently (if not entrepreneurship) with entrepreneurship? How do you intend to strike a balance?

2. Considering the current state of your country's economy, what are the opportunities presented for entrepreneurship?

3. What are the perceived challenges and how do you intend to overcome them?

NOTES

7

OTHER SHAME MONEY HEROES!

All over the world, there are several Shame Money stories. This was my conclusion when I decided to read up on successful entrepreneurs around the world. Let's see a few stories.

Sir Brian Souter

Sir Brian Souter is a Scottish billionaire and entrepreneur. He and his sister founded the Stagecoach Group of Bus and Rail Operators.

According to information on his website, www.briansouter.com , he had a love for buses right from childhood. His father was a bus driver, and Brian worked as a bus conductor when he was at the university. He would work in the morning, then go for his classes, and resume his bus conducting after lectures. After his university education, he got a job in an accounting firm in Glasgow but would still go bus conducting at weekends. His secret came out one

Monday morning when he appeared at the office with bruises all over his face; a violent passenger had beaten him up!

According to www.insider.co.uk, while travelling to Aberdeen, Brian discovered a shortage of intercity bus services and convinced his sister, Ann Gloag, and her husband to buy a bus. Brian bought two coaches in 1980 and that was the beginning of Stagecoach.

By 2010, he had about 13,000 coaches, buses, trains, and trams in the United Kingdom and North America and was providing employment to about 30,000 people in various countries around the world.

Mrs. Ayodeji Megbope

Mrs. Ayodeji Megbope is the CEO of No Leftovers, a catering outfit based in Nigeria.

How did she start her catering profession?

She worked at a school in Lagos, Nigeria for some years but wanted to do more with her life; so, she resigned from the school. Things became exceedingly difficult for her and her husband financially and, at a point, they found it difficult to feed themselves and the children.

One day, her husband gave her ₦1,000 (approximately $2) for food which was all he had. She thought of what to do with the ₦1,000. She said she heard God tell her to buy beans with the money. This she did. Mrs. Ayodeji took a part of the beans and made some moimoi (bean pudding). Her sister-in-law came visiting and she was served some moimoi. She commented on how tasty it was and requested that Mrs. Ayodeji make some for her, giving her ₦1,000.

That was how Mrs. Ayodeji's journey to entrepreneurship started. She realized she needed to make more sales but did not know how. She prayed about it and felt led to take her moimoi to the school where she used to teach. Mrs. Ayodeji stood at the gate and advertised to parents and teachers as they entered the school. It was a very humbling experience because people made fun of her. When people asked her why she left her paid job to sell moimoi, she would simply smile and continued to focus on her business. She decided that she would not allow negative comments to deter her, so she continued selling.

When some people tasted the moimoi, they started to ask her if she could make soups and stews, and she gladly agreed.

One day, she heard about a program for the empowerment of women entrepreneurs. It was sponsored by Goldman Sachs, an investment firm in the United States of America. She applied and won a scholarship to attend the program. Towards the end of the program, a delegation from Goldman Sachs came to interview her to showcase her story. They were inspired by her resilience and dedication. She subsequently got an invitation for a program in the United States of America for a few months and, soon afterwards, other invitations poured in.

In 2016, she was invited to speak at The United States of Women, a program in the United States of America. It was at this program that she got to serve her moimoi to the former First Lady of the United States, Michelle Obama, at the White House. She has since been invited by notable dignitaries around the world. She continues to inspire millions about overcoming shame in entrepreneurship and building a sustainable business.

Do Won Chang and Jin Sook Chang

The couple migrated to the United States of America from South Korea in 1981.

While trying to make ends meet in the United States, Do Won worked as a janitor in a coffee shop. He also went into the cleaning business while his wife worked as a hairdresser. He later secured a job at a clothing store so he could learn the basics of the business. Both were able to save up $11,000. With that amount, they started Fashion 21 in 1984.

They started this clothing retail store in Los Angeles with a floor space of about 84 square meters (900 square feet). Within a year, they generated a revenue of $700,000. With the growth in clientele, they changed the name to FOREVER 21. In 2015, FOREVER 21 witnessed a peak in sales to the tune of about $4.4billion.

Though FOREVER 21 filed for bankruptcy in 2019, their story is still an example of how much can be achieved with determination and passion even from very humble beginnings.

Michael Iloduba

Michael Iloduba is a Nigerian entrepreneur. He finished his secondary school education in 2013 but could not continue schooling due to lack of funds. He had to start work as a sales boy to save up some money.

Sometime in February 2019, he wore a suit and left the house in search of a better offer. He went from place to place and got tired of walking. When it was 4 p.m., he knew he could not continue walking and had to do something about his situation.

He was hungry, as he had not eaten all day and did not have enough money to take him back home.

Not minding that he was wearing a suit, Michael bought a bag of sachet water for ₦130. He did not have a bowl to sell with, so he had to rent one for ₦10. He went around advertising the water as 'corporate water' and sold out the twenty pieces he had in his bowl. He went back for some more water and soon enough, was able to sell fifty bags of water that day.

Today, he hawks sachet and bottled water dressed in corporate wear. This style of dressing, according to him, has been his primary marketing strategy.

Michael has featured on several TV shows where he encourages the youths to work instead of engaging in crime. He got his business name, Urban Corporate Water, registered with the Corporate Affairs Commission in October 2019 and has plans to scale up and expand.

John Paul Dejoria

John Paul DeJoria, an American billionaire, is the founder of tequila maker, Patron Spirits Co. He also co-founded John Paul Mitchell Systems. At a point in his life, John Paul slept in his car and sold encyclopedias door to door. He said this experience helped him learn how to deal with rejections.

He teamed up with his hairdresser, Paul Mitchell in 1980 and together they started John Paul Mitchell Systems, a haircare company, with just $700.

In 2017, his net worth was about $3.1 billion.

Joanne Rowling

This phenomenal author of the Harry Porter series battled depression, financial difficulties, grieving over the death of her mother and having to raise a child by herself while living on government benefits. At the end of a pretty difficult journey, she found comfort in working on her writing while her daughter slept.

Once the first few chapters of the book were complete, she sent the manuscripts to publishers, but her efforts were met with rejection. Her belief in what she had created helped her to persevere.

Finally, the Bloomsbury Publishing company agreed to publish the book but warned Rowling that she should get a day job because being a children's author was not enough to feed a family.

When the first book was released, it was evident no day job would be needed. Rowling was the first author to reach the billionaire mark, and her successful series has sold at least 500 million copies across the globe. The book series has made over $7.7 billion with the subsequent movies also bringing in money by the billions.

Her words of inspiration:

"You might never fail on the scale I did, but some failure in life is inevitable. It is impossible to live without failing at something, unless you live so cautiously that you might as well not have lived at all — in which case, you fail by default." -J.K. Rowling

NOTES

8

WHAT IS YOUR SHAME MONEY IDEA?

I believe everyone has an idea, a gift or talent that can be monetized. So, if you have been thinking of yourself as having nothing, you should change your mindset immediately. You have something important! The resource needed to implement your ideas and bring your passion to the forefront is a different topic entirely.

My reason for writing on a few Shame Money heroes is so you can see individuals, who were able to make something out of almost nothing, and know it is possible.

The way to discover what you have is by having a personal assessment. If you look carefully, you'll discover a need in the society that you have been wired to meet. Meeting this need could be through product sales or rendering services.

You should know that Shame Money is firstly about you, so your idea of making money this way should satisfy your primary stakeholder - YOU.

Self-satisfaction will prevent tension and mental exhaustion when you implement your idea.

Other questions to ask yourself in order to discover your Shame Money idea:

Does it bring out your creative prowess?

Does doing it make you want to do more and be better? Are you self-motivated and passionate about it? If you are not self- motivated about your idea, it is possible to fail even before you start and that is if you get started at all.

What are your personal traits?

Do you love music, organizing stuff, or entertaining people? Your passion might be in making people look beautiful or helping others to be their best. Some of these traits might be innate - they come to you naturally, and some might have been learnt unconsciously through different stages of your growth and development. You should pay attention and discover those that make you tick.

What do you enjoy doing but might be tasking?

Shame Money making for everyone does not have to be an easy path. You should ask yourself if you do not keep track of time when you are engaged in that activity. Is it

something you can do for hours, without getting
tired or bored?

Think about what you love doing. There should be one
thing that you don't mind doing from dawn to dusk; even
if you do not get paid for it.

Will I be paid for it?

Beyond pleasure or an interest in your idea, this is also
about money. Ask yourself if people will be willing to
pay you for that service. The fact that you may not be
getting paid for it right now does not mean people will
not pay for it in the future. It is also possible that you
have not been making any money because you have not
asked to be paid!

Shame Money making is doing something significant
for yourself instead of waiting for what society can do
for you. I strongly believe that if everyone were to
implement their Shame Money ideas, the problem of
unemployment would be seriously mitigated. With
dedication and commitment, the erstwhile unemployed
would not only be running their own businesses but
they would also be employing other people.

Implementing your Shame Money idea gives you a sense of fulfilment. Being able to do something of

value and being valuable to yourself and others will surely give you a form of indescribable joy.

Shame Money making is not just for 'broke' individuals. People who earn good monthly income can also take a cue from this. You do not have to resign from your place of work to begin; this can be a second source of income. You can monetize your gifts and ideas and make more money while still working your eight to five job. The fact that you do not have issues with your finances might even give you an edge; capital is assured, and you can start with your customer base which is your co-workers in your office.

What value will I be adding to society?

The more problems you are willing to solve, the more valuable you become. Shame Money is also about adding value. There are various problems in the society and your idea should be targeted towards solving one or more of these problems. You should ask yourself, "What problem(s) in the society will this provide a solution to?"

Talking in non-monetary terms, will you be adding value to the society? If you can answer this question in the affirmative, it might just be part of what will keep you going when you get discouraged during your Shame Money journey.

Let me give an illustration:

Sola is a biochemist by training but a roadside food seller by practice. Though he studied biochemistry at the university, he had been unsuccessful at getting a white- collar job for four years. Sola decided to take over his late mother's business of selling cooked food to commuters in the mornings. He had an advantage that he leveraged on: he was doing this in a very busy part of town where mothers rarely had the time to cook for their families before leaving the house in the mornings.

Some of Sola's former course mates at the University would come in their suits and briefcases, buy food from him, and take to their offices. Mothers would come, buy food for their families, and thank Sola for being of great help.

While running the business, he would sometimes feel discouraged and even contemplated quitting because of the shame of selling to his former colleagues.

What kept him going, however, was the thought of seeing the smiles on the faces of those he served, including mothers and children.

This is important. While this is Shame Money, it should not only be about the money; you should also have a great desire to add value. Do you love working with children and you think you can make money out of it? Why not start a playgroup? You might have a master's degree in Computer Engineering but starting a playgroup might be your Shame Money idea.

Discover your Shame Money idea, and you are on course to making some money.

ACTIONS POINTS

1. Why are you attracted to your Shame Money idea?

2. What value will you be adding to society when you execute your Shame Money Idea?

3. How viable is your Idea?

| |
| |
| |
| |

4. If it is not viable, what adjustments do you need to make so it becomes viable?

| |
| |
| |
| |

NOTES

9

While it is great to have ideas, plans, purposes and goals, it is even better to implement them. Your gifts and talents will remain innate and useless until you start to work with them. How do you run with your ideas?

Believe in Yourself

This is about you. If you believe this is what you can do, then you can do it. If you think otherwise, don't go into it. Believing in yourself will help you identify mistakes and find ways of correcting them without losing your passion.

Have a business plan

Write out your goals and objectives. Set timelines. Draw up a budget. A plan will keep you from losing focus. A goal is a standard to measure your progress.

You should also make sure that your bookkeeping/accounts are always in order. This will help you to know if you are making a profit and how much. Good bookkeeping might help you get funding or partners as your business grows.

Think carefully through your business plan.

Have a list of prospective customers

Who are your prospective customers? Make a list of people who may be interested in your product or services. If you are unable to think of at least 5 people in your network that might be interested in your product and services, then you might be barking up the wrong tree. How will you get it across to them? Have you worked out the logistics?

Be ready to adapt to change

Change, they say, is the only constant thing in life. You should have plans for handling changes when they come. These changes could be internal or external, and they have ways of affecting your business. Internal changes could be changes to your location while external changes could be changes to government policies that might affect your business.

You should be prepared to adapt to any of these changes when they come.

You should also stay updated on trends and your environment so you can easily spot and adjust to changes before your business starts to feel the impact.

Adapting to changes also involves changing your business strategies when you discover that the ones you are currently executing are not effective.

Have a success mindset

If you know the business is not going to be successful, why bother going into it? Be ready to take responsibility for your mistakes. Celebrate your achievements, no matter how little they are.

You will surely encounter challenges while implementing your ideas. Be ready to keep going instead of giving in to defeat. If you quit, you will never win.

Be willing to take risks

Entrepreneurship is not for the risk-averse; it is for risk-takers, the courageous and the most dogged people. Entrepreneurship involves taking risks, and you should be willing to take them, albeit, calculated risks. There is a probability that the business will fail and there are chances that you might have some losses, especially at the beginning. If this will happen is not the question; the question is "when you fall or the business fails, will you get back up and try again?" There are also chances that you will make some decisions that will affect your enterprise negatively. Will you let yourself drown in regret and personalize the failure, or will you pick the lessons and try again? It is completely up to you to decide.

Never give up on your dreams. You might not get it right at first. You might make some mistakes. You might lose your capital, but don't give up. Be willing to start all over again. See mistakes as opportunities to learn how not to do things.

Thomas Edison made about one thousand attempts while trying to invent the light bulb. When asked how he felt having failed a thousand times, he replied saying he didn't fail one thousand times, but the light bulb was an invention with one thousand steps.

Failure provides the opportunity to begin again, more intelligently.
~ Henry Ford.

Develop your Foresight

Our world has become a very fast-paced world with daily innovations, thereby changing the business world as we know it. As a business owner, it is imperative to stay on top of your game. Study your industry and the habits of your customers to enable you predict future trends. Train your mind to see the opportunities not yet saturated by your competitors. This is how to stay ahead of the game.

Hope for the best, prepare for the worst. This is part of your foresight skills. While you should have a positive attitude towards your endeavor, you should also be prepared for eventualities. Always be prepared for the worst-case scenarios. Have a plan for quick recovery. "If this happens, I am going to mitigate it with this, and I am going to bounce back."

Take advantage of technology

Social media platforms are not only for fun; they are great avenues to boost one's business at little or no cost
As at 2020, it is estimated that about 3.6 billion people are on social media all over the world.

People have built multimillion-dollar businesses through social media without a physical store. The long hours you spend browsing or chatting with friends can be channeled into doing something more productive, such as advertising your products online.

There are various social media platforms and the strategies for effective advertising on each platform might not be the same. You can learn how to optimize your social media handles to be able to get the best exposure for your products and services.

Get trained, add knowledge to your skill

You may not be the first person to venture into that business. However, adding knowledge to your skill base will make you stand out among competitors.

At inception, you might not have the financial capability to get trained in a formal environment, but you can learn in an informal environment. Practical knowledge is usually the best.

In the illustration given in the previous chapter, if Sola had not assisted his mum while she was alive, starting off the trade might have been daunting. He had to learn the basics before he started.

Sola did not have to go to a formal catering school; he only needed to volunteer as a worker in a restaurant to become familiar with running the business successfully. However, after a while, he could consider enrolling in a catering academy so he can do better in that sector.

Sourcing for Shame Money Capital

I think what makes Shame Money unique, is that little or no capital is needed to start the business enterprise. You may have to consider approaching friends and family for financial help.

I will advise you, as much as possible, not to take a loan. Do not start your Shame Money business with borrowed funds. The cost of loan repayment might weigh too heavily on you at the inception.

Hunger Will Keep You Going

If you don't have a passion for what you do, you are bound to fail at some point. In Shame Money, zeal and determination are particularly important in making things work.

Give yourself an inner push. Sit down and tell yourself why this should work. Get a notepad and highlight the reasons why your enterprise must be successful; and if you ever think of quitting, go back to your notepad and remind yourself why you must not quit.

You owe your future self a responsibility to grow that business and be successful at it.

ACTION POINTS

My free webinar 'How to Identify the source of your Shame Money' will among other things, help you identify obstacles that have held you back, how to overcome them, brainstorm the ideas you already have and go from thinking to execution.

To get started, visit www.shamemoney.com

1. What are your plans for successful entrepreneurship?

2. How do you intend to source for capital?

3. If you will be taking a soft loan, how do you intend to pay back without it affecting the business?

4. How fast or how big do you want your enterprise to grow? What can you do to make it happen?

5. Who is your target audience? How do you intend to get your products and services across to them?

NOTES

10

OVERCOMING THE 'WHAT-WILL-PEOPLE-SAY' MENTALITY!

Let's face it, this is what keeps most of us from daring to do more and better. *What will people say?* Many have given up on their dreams because they do not want to be castigated. Others have studied courses they should not have studied in a bid to please certain individuals.

While I will not dismiss the desire for social acceptance which is an innate desire in most people, we have to realize that social acceptance without self-acceptance can be disastrous.

How then do we overcome a fear of others' opinions? I think the answer simply is to love and appreciate yourself more than the opinions of other people about you.

Change your mind set

It begins with how you see your idea. You should start seeing your Shame Money idea as something you can do to add value to yourself and others, something you can do to feed your family, pay your bills, and something you can do to grow your income.

You might not be able to change the opinions of others, especially at the start of your enterprise, but please do not focus on them. Since you are the one who is going to implement and work on the idea, you should work on yourself first. How you see and perceive your idea will help you look beyond contrary opinions. See it positively.

Respect the dignity of labour

Working hard to make money should heighten your sense of responsibility. $1 earned through your sweat is often more valuable than $100 given to you as aid. If what you are doing is legal, no matter how physically 'dirty' it looks, you are doing a greatjob!

Who are your advisers? You need mentors to guide you, so you do not repeat the mistakes they made. You will no doubt make your own mistakes but having someone guide you provides immeasurable value. Be careful who you take counsel from. Talking to people about your business ideas and plans might be beneficial but do this with care. You do not have to seek counsel from everyone.

Some people are risk averse. They will, therefore, encourage you to have their perspective and avoid all forms of risk. You need to remember that entrepreneurship is not for the risk-averse but for people who will dare to do more.

Create a distance between yourself and bad energy. Some relationships might be detrimental or toxic to your Shame Money journey. Keep bad energy far from you and run from negative people. You have enough shame to deal with already; you do not need extra baggage.

No shame in your game

There is really nothing to be ashamed of. Yes! You are neither stealing nor doing anything illegal and that is enough to help you hold your head high.

Taking cues from some of our Shame Money heroes, how did they overcome their concern over people's opinions?

Mrs. Comfort Apata: She said she was not bothered. What mattered to her was that she was making money and was successful at it. She was determined to do something else asides from being a full-time mum.

Me: I refused to be deterred because I had a passion for what I was doing. It was not something illegal but a business that had to be accorded the respect it deserved. I knew I had to start small and work my way up, so I kept going.

Sir Brian Souter: Bus conducting was a need he saw in his environment which eventually became a passion. He 'named it, shamed it, and then famed it' to other countries.

Mrs. Ayodeji Megbope: The desire to feed her family trumped the shame of her selling moimoi (beans pudding). Each day was overwhelming. Today, she has a chain of restaurants. She reminded herself of dignity of labor and decided to turn a blind eye to people ridiculing her.

Mr. Michael Iludobah: He decided not to be bothered about the opinion of others. He did not complain or beg for temporary relief, instead, he was determined to creatively make something of himself.

For anyone who chooses to venture out, no doubt, the sky is the beginning.

ACTION POINTS

1. This is a practical activity I will recommend that you do repeatedly. Go to the front of your mirror, look at your reflection and say to yourself; "I am proud of the good works of my hands. There is no shame in honest labor therefore I am never ashamed of my Shame Money business. I thank God for giving me beautiful ideas to bless my world with. I am grateful for my Shame Money ideas and I execute them boldly".

2. Will you quit if there are discouragements from unexpected sources or people closest to you look down on your idea as unbefitting to your status?

3. Why do you believe so much in your Shame Money idea and why would you keep going despite all the discouragements you will encounter?

NOTES

11

ACCORD YOURSELF THE RESPECT OF GROWTH

Shame Money is not a get-rich-quick magic wand and you should not start seeing it as one, otherwise you are in for a rude shock as you might not strike gold immediately.

Having a Shame Money idea and putting it to work does not guarantee success. Yes, you read that right. Money should be made and made to grow. If you do not take steps towards making your Shame Money grow, you will end up frustrated.

Growth does not happen overnight; it takes time. This is where a lot of people get it wrong. They start quite well but lack what it takes to keep going. Some of them give up and dismiss it all as 'mere motivational talk' that cannot be put into practice.

You should create processes and introduce structures to enable the business scale up by continually revising your strategies to meet up with current realities. Do not ever get tired of acquiring knowledge or adjusting to change.

Work Hard

A lazy person won't make a good Shame Money entrepreneur. At inception, you may be the only one doing everything necessary to run the business. Be ready to work hard.

It is a lot of work and you do not want to be merely going through the motions each day. Be clear in your mind that it is hard work and you are going to do it all the same.

Break up big tasks into little ones and set a time limit for each one. Reward yourself when you achieve critical milestones. Take very good care of your health; you will achieve more when you are healthy than when you are not.

Genius is one percent inspiration and ninety-nine percent perspiration.
~Thomas Edison

Skill Up

Humans need the right set of nutrients to grow. In Shame Money, growth entails developing the right skill set to boost your business.

What are the skills needed to succeed as a Shame Money entrepreneur?

Financial intelligence

You should be familiar with skills under financial intelligence such as accounting, bookkeeping, budgeting etc.

Some people are naturally prudent: they earn more, spend some, save some, and invest the rest. Some are natural spenders: they earn less, spend some and maybe save with no investment. Some people fall in between.

These habits have ways of affecting your business and might have been picked up from people in your circle of influence.

It does not matter if you are prudent or lavish, everyone needs to learn financial intelligence. If you already think you have financial intelligence, you should continue to sharpen it.

Leadership skills

You will need to organize people and resources towards achieving your enterprise's goals and you need some leadership skills to make this happen.

You should work on being creative, reliable and patient. Learn to listen to your employees and customers so you can genuinely understand their concerns before speaking. Other leadership skills you need to work on are dependability, empathy, team building, strategic thinking, and time management skills.

Your ability to develop, encourage and motivate your staff will go a long way in aiding your ability to inculcate desired work policies and ideals.

Interpersonal skills

What is a business without customers? Knowing how to relate to customers will not only help you to keep them, it will also help you to keep getting referrals. You should be able to connect with people easily.

Get feedback from your customers on a constant basis. It will help you to know what their needs are, what you are doing well, and the areas you need to improve on.

Persuasive skills

Persuasion is not manipulation; it is helping people

make decisions that are beneficial to them. You need to know how to get people to buy into your ideas. Some people will not buy your products or require your services unless you make them see why they should do so.

Note: You don't need to be proficient in these skills before you start; you can pick them up as you go.

Take Opportunities

Several opportunities will surface during your Shame Money journey. These opportunities might include getting more knowledge, funding from the government or private individuals, partnerships or investment opportunities. While maximizing them might be the much- needed boost to propel your business forward, missing out on such opportunities might push you out of business.

While I do not believe opportunities come once, I will also caution against thinking opportunities are constantly around you. Some wonderful opportunities may come to us in three-piece suits and matching shoes, while others may come disguised in tattered clothes and bare feet.

An entrepreneur's success lies in seeing beyond the

physical to analyze and maximize opportunities, some of which may not be there perpetually. There will be times we would really need to shut our ears to external voices and listen to the voice deep within.

As a Shame Money entrepreneur, you will be required to make some firm decisions in dealing with various opportunities when they come.

Dare to stand out!

Our brains have been programmed in such a way that makes it easy for us to quickly spot a red card in a pack of white cards. Standing out involves going the extra mile, taking extra care to do what others are not doing and paying attention to minute details. This is what will get you easily noticed amidst the multitude.

Build your Shame Money enterprise to stand out by doing common stuff in uncommon ways. Beating competitors is easier when, through focusing on you and not just your competitors, you are able to create a unique feature.

Save and Invest Your Profit

Don't squander your profits. You can reinvest it in the business or diversify into other businesses. You should not go ahead to change your wardrobe because you just made a big profit. You should have ready plans on how to manage your profits; it should not be something you do impulsively.

Will all the profits be channeled back into the business? Will some be set aside to allow for diversification? Will you save some in the money market or treasury bills?

Take some time to answer questions like these ahead of time. You do not have to be rigid about it; you can always make changes to reflect current realities.

For a Shame Money entrepreneur, savings and investments are sure ways of growing your business faster. While you are doing your best to increase proceeds from the business, you could also have the profits of that business growing in the money market.

How About Some Poise?

Do not invoke self-pity. Your carriage should speak of excellence. When 'sympathizers' accost you (they inevitably will), you should be gentle but very firm with them. You don't need a pity-party and you surely don't need their sympathy. What you need is their patronage, and you should make them realize that.

Carry yourself in such a way that people will want to do what you do. Dress like you are worth a billion dollars. Speak like you have the world at your feet for the taking. Confidence is not pride or rudeness, rather, it stems from knowing what you want and going for it without an apology.

ACTION POINTS

1. What are your strategies for growing your enterprise?

2. How do you intend handling growth and expansion?

3. How do intend to skill up?

a. (Short term) Plans to take up free online courses or available free trainings.

| |
| |
| |
| |

b. (Long term) Plans to get more knowledge in a formal environment.

| |
| |
| |
| |

4. How do you intend to manage your profit?

| |
| |

5. What are the skills you need to acquire or improve on?

6. How and when do you intend to start working
   on those skills?

7. What do you understand by reinvesting your capital?

8. What are the various means of investments available
   to you as a starting entrepreneur?

12

The essence of this book is not to fill your mind with theories or principles that cannot be practiced. Its purpose is to get you on your feet and help you break free from the mindset struggles holding you back from pursuing that business idea that might be what you need to change the tides of your finances.

Much more than the possibility of a financial turnaround that Shame Money holds, it is also a path of tremendous growth. When you execute your idea, you will be surprised at how fast and how well you will grow. Entrepreneurship will teach you so much and force you to grow in every sense of it. This is one of the reasons why I personally love entrepreneurship.

Entrepreneurship will teach you to: rise above failure; Multi-task, think on your feet, manage crisis, manage people; improve your emotional intelligence; and push yourself more than you thought was possible.

Telling the story of Mrs. Comfort Titilayo in this book, might have made her story look so seamless. It may have seemed like everything was just falling into place. Please do not be deceived! There were a lot of failures, disappointments and heartbreaks that this book can never possibly contain, but as with every success story, the whole picture will always look so beautiful when looking in from outside.

So, at the point where you face challenges or setbacks on your journey, or you just don't know how everything will work together to bring that beautiful vision you have seen in your mind to reality, just have faith and trust in your process. One day you will look back too and see the whole picture; and it will be beautiful, I have no doubts!

For the action points at the end of the chapters, I encourage you to take your time with them. Think deeply on those questions and answer honestly. They were designed to help you overcome the barriers in your mind and bring you to the point of action.

My greatest joy will be to hear your story of how this book helped you overcome the hurdles in your mind that stopped you from embracing your Shame Money and how you triumphed beautifully.

I would like to hear from you.

You can share with me how applying the principles in this book has helped you grow your Shame Money idea. If you also need personal coaching in going about your Shame Money idea, I will be glad to help.

Simply send me a message on Instagram. Our handle is @Shamemoneyorg.

Best wishes on your journey.

I am rooting for you!

ABOUT THE AUTHOR

Motunrayo Ade-Famoti is the CEO of Moneystewards, an Investment firm located in Texas, USA. Moneystewards, has expertise in foreign investments and invests in a diverse portfolio of paper assets and several real estate projects in the USA.

She has travelled and worked extensively around the world. She started investing in London real estate and emerging markets over 20 years ago. She is the founder of "Shame Money Movement", an organization that assist SME's and lower income bracket families start a business and provide access to funding.

She is a speaker at several investment and real estate conferences, an author, a financial coach, and a mentor. She founded the "Mentorship with Mo" program which focuses on helping young professionals grow their money management skills. She is extremely passionate about her Foundation, "feeding the slums" where she feeds families living in some of the worst slums in Africa.

She holds a law degree from University of Sheffield, UK. Legal Practice Course from Inns of Court, School of Law, London and a Master's in International Law from City University, London. She is a Solicitor and Commissioner for Oath of the Supreme Court of England and Wales and an Attorney at law at New York State, USA.